G000081136

ENGLISH COUNTRY
TRADITIONS

ENGLISH COUNTRY TRADITIONS

WOOD ENGRAVINGS BY
CHRISTOPHER WORMELL

WRITTEN BY
IAN NIALL

RUNNING PRESS
PHILADELPHIA · LONDON

British Library Cataloguing-in-Publication Data.
A catalogue record for this book
is available from the British Library.

ISBN 1–56138–692–8

This book may be ordered by mail from the publisher.
Please include £1.00 for postage and handling.
But try your bookstore first!

Running Press Book Publishers
Cedar House
35 Chichele Road
Oxted, Surrey RH8 0AE

FOR MARY

CONTENTS

FOREWORD

Christopher Wormell has long been active as a wood engraver and has not only established himself as a master in the medium but also made a place for it in contemporary graphics as a force to be reckoned with. Son of a landscape painter, he left school at 18 in 1973 to support himself in a variety of jobs while devoting himself to painting. He has always greatly admired the work of the father of the English wood engraving tradition, Thomas Bewick (1753–1828), whose blocks he remembered seeing as a child in the V & A. In 1982, visits to the exhibition of work by Reynolds Stone (1900–1979) in the

National Art Library at the V & A confirmed his resolution to develop his interest in a medium then generally considered in terms of its historic achievements.

There can be no doubt that wood engraving enjoyed a revival in the mid-1980s, one that continues unabated today. We see it in the activities of the Society of Wood Engravers, established in 1920 by Robert Gibbings, Noel Rooke, Eric Gill and others, which seemed to draw increasing attention to itself after the arrival of Hilary Paynter in 1984. Christopher Wormell's career testifies to the same revival of interest. His first work as an engraver was for Faber & Faber, a book cover for

Brian Friel's play *The Communication Cord*, followed by a design for Seamus Heaney poems and other commissions. Perhaps what really launched Christopher Wormell's work was the series of illustrations he provided for the series 'British Cookery' in the *Observer* newspaper's colour magazine early in 1984. Today he can look back on a series of commissions done for an impressively wide range of clients, from Jonathan Cape and Penguin to the *Radio Times*, *The Times*, Goldcrest Films, David Puttnam and Saatchi and Saatchi.

Christopher Wormell is evidently most at home when providing illustrations for a text published in a book. He had long admired the writings of Ian

Niall before meeting him in the winter of 1985–6 to discuss the work published in the following pages. Wormell followed his mentors Bewick and Stone in reserving his best work for the English landscape. Who more suitable than Niall, author of *The Poacher's Handbook* and *A Galloway Childhood*, to say nothing of the *Portrait of a Country Artist* commemorating his friend Charles Tunnicliffe, to provide texts from which the wood engraver could take his cue.

Elizabeth Esteve-Coll
Director of the Victoria and Albert Museum, 1988

IT IS NOT RECORDED that Adam kept bees in the Garden of Eden but man has indeed kept bees for a very long time treating them with less respect than the modern up-to-date apiarist when, to steal the honey, he did not hesitate to destroy his colony.

The townsman is less likely to be able to accommodate a beehive on his premises, but since time immemorial the cottager has kept bees. Looking after apiaries was part of the labour of monks. The Romans were advised on the management of bees by the poet, Virgil, and honey has always been credited with

Beehives

wonderful healing properties as well as having great benefit to the person who takes it by the spoonful to soothe a cough.

Today, few mysteries concerning the life of the bee remain unsolved. The humblest cottager when he goes to 'take the honey off' knows from books just what the system he is disturbing is all about, but the taste of honey depends on the season. If there was an early spring and a great abundance of blossom the beekeeper may taste honey that came from the apple tree overlaid, perhaps, with sycamore and a touch of the field maple. Later his honey, if he lives within reach of moorland, will be dark and heavy, a gathering from ling and heather.

By examining the progress of honey gathering the cottager can decide for himself when it is time to take his honey. He never dares take it all unless he is prepared to replace it with a gallon or two of sugar either in liquid form or candy. Honey has the same quality as wine. It never can be exactly the same again because that precise sequence of summer days will never be repeated.

HERE HAS ALWAYS
been a tendency to
conjure up a romantic
picture of the reaper
in the rye grass. With
the enchantment of
nostalgia, hay-making
was all a kind of picnic under a heaven-
ly sky and the twittering flights of
swallow and martin high above it all.
On the hay scented field, butterflies
settled to sun themselves and the grass-
hopper sang endlessly. Such idylls
are made of fond memory of the heat
haze and happy, laughing people lounging after their labours by the tea
basket. They were always surrounded
by wild snapdragons, meadowsweet

Hay-making

that was almost over-powering in its sweetness, and delicate hairbells that swayed in the gentle breeze. Time was marked by thistledown sailing silently up, and away.

The reality was something quite different. The hay-maker watched anxiously for the rain cloud. A downpour meant that all his labour would be undone. The gathered swath would have to be forked or raked apart again. In its wet state it couldn't be carted into the rickyard or the barn.

The raking and turning would go on day after day, week after week. It wasn't the picnic that kept the peasant family working in the field but sheer desperation. It could all be made worse by biting insects and the awful irritation when small seeds worked their way down into a man's heavy woollen vest. When the first raindrops began to spatter down, long-bodied rainflies emerged from the ditch to drink blood and inflict severe pain. After a little while it would all become unbearable as well as futile. A hayfield never was a place for anyone who couldn't go on, but had to lie on his back while the sun shone and he admired that sheepflock of far-up white clouds.

EVERYONE WHO HAS ever gone mushrooming learns that some fields are better than others. The old countryman knows even more—those places he harvests year after year. His special field is a most closely guarded secret. He is careful to pick it bare so that not a single cluster of mushrooms remains to advertise what a latecomer might expect if he could force himself to leave his bed early enough and venture forth into the dawn. Long before the traffic has begun to destroy the holy peace of early morning, the mushroomer who knows his business is out

Wild Mushrooms

and back home again with mushrooms tastier than anything the professional grower can ever hope to produce in his dark barn or basement.

The field that grows the real mushroom is one long lain fallow or never ploughed at all. It is an ancient pasture of rich, deep turf that ponies have grazed, a place sheltered a little from the fiercest of the sun's heat in an Indian summer, if such a late summer there has been. In the rich loam in which the wholesome grass roots find nourishment spores of the fungus have fallen. The tracery of mycelium, branching again and again, and more beautiful than the most delicate work of the lace-maker, spreads and gives rise, quite literally, to the mushroomer's breakfast feast. The common field mushroom, alas, is where the average mushroom gatherer draws his line, although both fields and woods abound in similar delicacies, some less appetising than the great horse mushroom that stains the gravy black, and others, like the morel and the blusher, highly prized by the expert chef.

IT CAN'T BE SAID THAT the ploughman's world was ever entirely idyllic. His landship, as the horseplough was sometimes called, cut a furrow through cow-slips and yarrow, vetch and thistle, leaving behind it a smooth, evenly ironed furrow over which yelping gulls sailed or glided. With the passing of months the whole surface of the former pasture became a wonderful pattern of straight furrows boxed by a ploughed headland on which, in due time, peewits might nest and mad March hares sport themselves.

The Plough

When it was all done, the ploughman skidded his plough to the implement shed and brought out the harrows and the roller. Summer came, with haymaking before corn harvest, and there he was, back again, ploughing out the potato crop with the ridger or hiller, and actually looking forward to the long walk once again with the occasional ploughing match to brighten the darker days of November. Without his labour the sower, who walked the furrows broadcasting corn by the handful, or scattering it with a device called a 'fiddle', would have nothing to do, nor would he himself be there to gather peewits' eggs in spring, sending them to hotels in the big cities to provide a very special treat for their wealthier patrons. They might not have been all jolly fellows who followed the plough, but they took great pride in their work and loved their horses, grooming and feeding them at the end of every day— always before they even thought of going for their own supper. It is sad that the painted-up plough on the pub forecourt tells nothing of this.

ARTRIDGES ARE
never very con-
spicuous birds;
for, although
they occasional-
ly roost in the
thorn trees of a
low-growing,
thick hedge in
winter, they are ground birds in the
true sense. Hatched in the long grass
or in the bramble bush on the hedge
bank, they have the ability to get up
and go soon afterwards. Never need-
ing to be fed by their parent, they
escape the attention of predators like
the brown rat who, having found a
feast of eggs, returns to the nest again

Partridges

and again until he has taken them all.

The little brown birds of the furrows, as they have been called, have always been hunted. Man used to net the partridge covey by walking the field in which it settled to roost for the night and dropping his net over them. The gun enabled him with the aid of setters or pointing dogs to shoot the covey, one by one, as it flew on to settle and be discovered again by its relentless pursuers. The game laws protected the partridge from the poacher and left it to the mercy of the landowner. Some land-owners loved partridge shooting so much that their keepers were instructed to gather the eggs, bring them on under a broody hen, and take them back to hatch naturally under the bird that had laid them. This was achieved by leaving the wild partridge dummy eggs to sit on while her own eggs were protected both from predators and the cold rain in a bad summer. Partridges decline in numbers in bad years and landowners lament that the native bird (the red-legged partridge seen in the southern counties is also known as a Frenchman) is dying out in some places.

IN DAYS GONE BY, WHEN, apart from those Roman roads Britain had inherited from the Caesars, communications between county towns and market towns and villages beyond were poor indeed, farmers who grew wheat, barley or oats needed to have their grain harvest milled to provide themselves with flour and oatmeal. The mill had to be within reasonable distance from the farm, about as far as a team could haul a wagon there and back again. The journey to the mill would be painful and demanding when the terrain was hilly.

The Journey to the Mill

The economy of the arable farmer made it essential that he got his grain harvest through the mill and onto the market as quickly as possible. Cities depended on the corn grown in their immediate vicinity and the miller was an important cog in the wheel. Flour went to local bakeries. If man didn't live by bread alone it was still the staff of life, and many poor people had little else on which to keep body and soul together. Year in, year out, the jolly miller kept the grindstone grinding. The village baker baked his bread. In farmhouses in places where no wheat was grown, sacks of flour were kept in bunkers to make what today is still called farmhouse bread. The flour was once traded for oats at the local mill, and the remainder of the oat crop fed to horses, pigs and fowl. This was part of a closely integrated economy in which flour milling was particularly important.

Today, the many hundreds of flour mills that once dotted the length and breadth of Britain are reduced to a few curiosities. Milling has been centralised. Derelict waterwheels are to be found in waterless sluices. Skeleton sail mills, most with their timbers rotting, are renovated and restored from time to time to make tourist attractions. Harvested grain now goes from silos to the milling centre. The day of the working windmill and watermill is over.

HEN WILLIAM Cobbett surveyed the counties of England and gave an account in his celebrated *Rural Rides*, he deplored the decline in the numbers of congregations at country churches. In the early decades of the nineteenth century the rural population was in decline. Churches were showing signs of neglect. The rural population had filtered away as men found jobs created by the industrial revolution.

Country folk had been, in the main, God-fearing and devoted to their church. As ever, the country church

The Country Church

remains in many places the focal point for worship and social contact. With a congregation spread more thinly on the ground than that of his counterpart in the market town, the rector knows not only the faces of his flock, but their most intimate affairs.

Come harvest festival the women bring flowers, generally the flowers of their own cottage gardens, and decorate the church from porch to altar. Their menfolk fork the vegetable garden to dig up and carefully select their finest potatoes, carrots, parsnips or beetroot, all of them presented with as much care as for the annual flower and vegetable show. Where the art of making a corn dolly still survives, there will be beautifully plaited stalks of wheat, executed by someone to whom this art has been handed down by father or grandfather. Harvest home is not, of course, the only time the ladies of the congregation get together to decorate the church. The porch has hardly been tidied up and the aisles swept before they are back at work decorating it over again for Christmas and helping to build that minor work of art, the thatched manger with the holy infant. These customs are as old as the churches themselves.

THE DITCH THAT RUNS along the boundary of the hedge bank is as important to the condition of the pasture as it is to the health and productivity of the cultivated field. Into this open drain run the land drains of red clay tiles or more ancient draining systems of stone, rubble or even brushwood.

The ditch may serve as a watering hole for cattle. It may shelter waterbirds like the wagtail and the water hen that find nesting places along its course. The yellowhammer may nest on the hedge bank above with the

The Ditcher

hedgesparrow, and the ditch, where it broadens, provide a minor pool or pond where a pair of wintering teal will swim, and mallards paddle to dip for weed. Ditches or fen drains may also support fish, the loach and the eel, which the old grey heron will hunt. Frogs and toads emerge from the weeds and freshwater shrimps live in a swaying forest of cress and duckweed.

As time goes by the ditch slowly fills with decaying vegetable matter and dead wood. It had to be cleaned out and the traditional way was for the ditcher to come along with his long-handled shovel and scoop out everything, throwing it all onto the bank.

The ditcher's work was seasonal and generally done between harvests, never in 'February fill-dyke' when there is always a flood or spate, but when it was important to improve the drainage of an arable field to be put under the plough again or bear the weight of cornbinder or wagons. The old time ditcher may have loved his work and enjoyed shovelling out the eel or getting himself a few crayfish for supper, but he has long since been replaced by his modern counterpart—a relentless mechanical monster.

EDGES MAY BE DIS-appearing from the rural landscape at the rate of several thousand miles a year. Thousands of miles of ancient hedge have been grubbed up since the present century began. There is nothing like the green thorn tree, the briar, and the tough old blackthorn, for discouraging animals from breaking out of their field. Hedges require that much more atten-tion than drystone walls, for the thorn will grow higher and leave gaps that animals may push through.

The Hedger

The hedger's trade was often linked to the ditcher's, both having their seasons. His tools were the hedgeknife and the billhook. Armed with these he would make his way steadily from one corner of the field to the next, slashing the briar and topping the thorn so that it would grow bushier, sparing the ash sapling and the young field maple to grow into hedge trees in due time. Here and there he would be forced to do a stretch of fencing, hopefully leaving the young thorns to weave themselves into a permanent barrier and keep out a neighbour's ill-provided-for sheep or horses. Time makes a hedge and, while the hedge may draw nourishment from the headland as its roots spread farther into the field, it also provides shelter for the wintering flock and beasts that would otherwise starve in the east wind. Even the arable field derives some benefit from the windbreak.

Hedge-laying is a skill that is now rare. There is no better barrier, but it can't be done to every hedge, except by a millionaire. It is one of the rural crafts that is also an art, but, sadly, one practised by fewer and fewer men as the years pass.

OTTAGE GARDENS are never entirely beds of roses with lavender bushes and pink-flowering currants that shelter fluffed-up bantams. The garden may have its lavender and thyme, its gilly flowers, hollyhocks and delphiniums. Tea rose and honeysuckle may drench the evening air with their perfume while turtle doves purr, but behind the ancient dwelling lies the vegetable garden with perhaps an old apple or an old pear tree that still bears a fair crop in a good season. Here the soil has been continually enriched and improved until

The Cottage Garden

it might be dug with bare hands, so deep and good is its tilth. Hundredweights of manure and humus of different origins have gone into it to produce an unbelievable yield of King Edwards or Arran Pilot. No finer carrots are grown by any professional. Parsnips there are to lie on the cottager's plate and make his mouth water, and there are beetroots, onions and shallots. The rhubarb patch is for jam-making. Fat marrows break from their covering of long-stemmed leaves and, if there are weeds—chickweed and groundsel for the birds—it is only because the cottager hasn't enough hours in his day to do everything that needs to be done in his garden.

Labour in his garden is a labour of love and he forgets the backache, working for himself, making his own potato clamp, bringing in his own harvest of carrots and storing them against the frost. In harder times the garden was often all that stood between the family and penury, but even in the day of packaged food and the deep freeze nothing the cottager eats can taste half as good as the things he grows and harvests by the sweat of his brow. No piece of ground means more to him.

THATCH IS WITHOUT doubt one of the oldest ways employed by man to keep a dry roof over his head. With luck a well-thatched roof might last for even seventy years. In this time the sedge ridge-covering will have been renewed regularly and sections of the eighteen inches' thick, double layer of reed or wheat straw, showing signs of letting water in, will have been redone by the skilled thatcher. The most vulnerable part of the 'butted' reed or straw is the end of the material, the place where it may not

Thatching

only rot, but be attacked by the pests that plague the life of anyone living under an old thatch. Birds remorselessly pull out straws and strive to make a hole so that they can nest in the attic or build an equally snug nest in the cavity they have made. Rats may follow in due course and, once a thatched roof begins to slump, there is no remedy but to get the thatcher back on the job.

A first-class thatch is usually fastened to the rafters by means of hooks, driven in to hold down the reed after the thatcher has located the position of the support by probing. The process of laying on begins at the eaves and is carried upwards, layer after layer held down by hazel rods, and each bundle of thatch is thoroughly beaten to ensure an even butt. Rain must run down the butt from ridge to eaves without seeping into the covering as a whole. Insurance may be expensive and frequent maintenance necessary, but there is much to be said for living in fairyland and waking to the twittering of birds immediately above one's bed.

SINCE THE FIRST FIELD was delineated, and man found it necessary to keep things in while keeping others out, he has been a waller, builder of pens and sheepfolds from boulders near to hand, quarrying local stone to enclose more and more ground.

He would use the stones ploughed from his field to reinforce his old walls or sometimes build them into new walls with clods of earth, a fashion regularly employed in Devon. Cotswold stone is famous and there is nothing more handsome than a perfectly built

Walling

wall of Cotswold stone. Like limestone, Cotswold quarried stone lends itself to regular construction. A template is employed to make sure the contour is maintained on any particular stretch of wall being put up, the completed wall may then be topped with coping stones. In limestone and mortar walls encountered in parts of North Wales, the containing stonework is filled in with limestone rubble, broken limestone or quarry residue particularly suitable as a core. The coping stones, solidly mortared in place, discourage the most agile sheep or goat from climbing out of, or into the ground enclosed. The only danger to the solid structure that may finally bring it tumbling down is when humus accumulates between the coping stones and seeds germinate. Plants like valerian or elder, taking root, force their way down and dislodge the coping. When this happens, and the roots find more room, they may burst the wall and the rubble within spills out.

The waller's craft is fast dying. There are no apprentices. Few can afford to build in stone. The craft is revived and encouraged by drystone walling competitions, but very few of the entrants earn their living building new drystone walls.

HERE BUT IN THE country would there be room for the old orchard? The professional orchardsman may have a forest of healthy young trees bearing the maximum crop because his well-ordered plantation has been fertilised and his trees carefully pruned, banded and sprayed at exactly the right time. Alas, the average countryman watches his precious tree grow old and gnarled, and every five or six years has a crop to make up for the years between when it gave him only a hatful of apples to stew with a handful of blackberries and make into a pie.

Apple Picking

The old tree shades a corner of the garden. In twisted and interlocking branches that should have been cut out with a pruning saw, a mistlethrush or a collared dove builds a nest. When the old tree bears its crop in a year of plenty, so does the cross-pollinator close by, as well as the tree beyond that, planted even earlier by the cottager who loved apple trees, but never thought about his capacity to eat apple pie or apple dumpling. A hundred apples fall to the grass.

Most of the old orchard trees have lost their names. A few may be identified by old men who remember the taste of a once highly thought-of variety. One or two go into decline without ever being identified except as the apple 'old missis so-and-so' made her apple jelly from. Occasionally the countryman who knows very little about root pruning or ring-barking will load his shotgun and shoot the old tree that hasn't had an apple on it for years. Sometimes a miracle results and the tree bears fruit, the shotgun wound doing exactly what ring-barking would have done.

A VARIETY OF CHURNS may be seen in old farm museums. Barrel churns were rotated by a crank and had a milk-tight, or cream-tight lid. Cream turns to butter when the fat content of the milk separates from the rest. The end products are butter and buttermilk, and the process is not unlike cheese-making which results in separating curd from whey. Turning the churn at an even speed eventually brings about the golden nuggets of butter in thinned buttermilk. The operator watches for this in a little glass window that at first carries a film of milk and then gradually clears to become

The Butterchurn

speckled soon afterwards with tiny flecks of butter. When the window is clear again and the butter nuggets are beginning to amalgamate, the lid of the churn is unscrewed and the buttermilk strained off through a muslin cloth. The process is yet far from completion for the churned butter has to be beaten until all liquid, buttermilk and water, has been forced out. Finally, the carefully measured and weighed pats of butter are wrapped for market, some of them decorated by means of a mould leaving the imprint of perhaps a rose, a thistle, or a sheaf of wheat.

All this, and the skill of the dairymaid, has disappeared from the scene in fifty or sixty years. The factory began to take over when the first vegetable oil product called margarine began to appear on the market. Dairy farmers scornfully dubbed it refined axle grease and doubted its future, little thinking that in a short time the focus of the dairy industry would be in vast plants designed to take the labour out of butter churning, and, some people still insist, the real taste out of country butter!

THERE IS HARDLY A country parish in rural Britain without a lake, pond, stream, meandering or turbulent river in which fish of one aspect or another are found. Some of the brooding ponds in remote places contain carp, bream or pike and perch, fish that are thought little of by the cook in modern times. The carp is a classic example of the stewpond fish brought to this country so that the monastery could have its fish on Friday; but, when communications were so poor, any kind of fish, muddy-tasting or not, was welcomed

Fishing

on the labourer's table. If his master fished for the lordly salmon and reserved the fishing on the chalk stream for himself, because the brown trout was much more to his liking than what are known as coarse fish, the peasant went forth with a makeshift rod and perhaps no reel, or 'wheel', at all with which to play his pike or perch. The garden worm or the entrails of a fowl were good enough bait and necessity forbade any pre-occupation with what might have been considered sporty and what was not. In the sixteenth century few of the fishermen who sought sport on either the great salmon rivers of the north or the idyllic reaches of Itchen, Test of Kennet thought of finer fishing rods and the design of the reel. Such things took their time. Great brown trout swam in the mill pools or had their moorings in green jungles of waterweed through which pure rivers flowed. God was in the fisherman's heaven. The bittern boomed in the reeds, and kingfishers fished while the colley bird, the whitebibbed dipper, walked into the torrent and the very heart of the flood to get food for its nestlings under the bridge.

VEN IN THE FAR-OFF days when an ordinary man who put up a gun to shoot a pheasant risked transportation to the Antipodes without a return-trip ticket available to him after he had served his seven years, wildfowling tended to be in a class of its own. The great landowner might lay claim to the riverbank, the estuary and even the shore, but below highwater mark the commoner might get himself a wintering wigeon or a goose. In the wilderness of East Anglian marshes, as near jungle as could be found in the British Isles, the old professional

Wildfowling

fowlers plied their trade and cultivated skills that enabled them to make great bags of different sorts of fowl that were readily bought by London merchants.

This trade was seasonal, of course, because it depended upon the north-south migrations of certain species. Geese came in from Greenland and Iceland, from Scandinavia and the ice wastes of Russia. Ducks came in thousands to shelter in the long lanes of reeds and the minor lakes and bays of lowland waterways in the Broads. It wasn't that the landowner didn't appreciate the natural bounty that he might have claimed as exclusively his. Wild-fowling always had a degree of hardship, acute suffering at times, for the man stalking his prey among frozen reeds and through icy pools.

Wildfowl, it was agreed, almost without saying, were fair enough game for the 'shore popper' and the marsh creeper who paddled his skiff into the mist and lined up his cannon of a fowling piece, his very breath freezing in his beard as he did so. The punt gun has now gone to the museum. The present-day fowler may arm himself with a repeating shotgun but must content himself with a much smaller bag.

THE BEST CIDER COMES from those southern parts of Great Britain where cider apples have always been grown. The traditional west country product was mainly brewed for home consumption and known as rough or scrumpy. This may still be bought in a west country pub, and many an innocent holidaymaker has succumbed to its delayed-action effect. It can be as potent as strong ale, and leave a nasty headache the following day. The apple harvest is a 'back-end' event and it makes little difference to the final product whether the apples

Cider-making

fallen into the orchard grass were bruised or turned brown.

Their destination is the cider mill, generally a piece of ancient equipment that may be hand-operated, or powered by a sturdy workhorse on a 'walk' mill. Whether the apples are crushed by more sophisticated means, or put through the old mangle, the object is to produce pomace from which the apple juice will be pressed, strained, and finally siphoned off to be fermented, a process that may take a week or ten days. Straining in the first instance may be through hessian. In some cases straw is also used, although straw can give an unwanted flavour to the end product. Even the pressed-out juice will be nothing like that crystal-clear commercially produced glass of branded cider and, when it goes into the casks, casks that once held wine or spirit, where the final ferment takes place, impurities will surge in the cloth-stopper bung-hole. These will be cleared and the barrel re-stoppered in the same way after the vessel has been topped up. This topping up is essential to the production of drinkable rough or sweet cider, or vinegar will result. Rough cider was almost everywhere the west country farmer's substitute for home-brewed beer.

I F AN ENGLISHMAN'S home is his castle, beer is his favourite drink. There is no drink quite like it. What has saddened the dedicated beer drinker most in recent years is an intervention of the chemist between himself and the master brewer, the man who put the hops in his pint and produced good bitter beer. Alas for the chemist, the rude forefathers of the village were not all gone to their long rest. Some had sat on the very same settle when the landlord himself had served them with a pint of best, brewed on the premises! It had

The Hopfield

been real strong stuff, tuppence a pint. Young lads had fallen about groping for the sneck of the door when they had had no more than two pints of it. What the marketing experts overlooked was nostalgia. Beer had always been cheaper, stronger, and had more body in it. It had real hops in it. Everyone knew that chemists were imitating the flavour of the hop. How long was it since anyone had found a hop in the pintpot?

'Real' ale was a device the small brewer employed to steal a share of the market. A good pint was a well-kept pint. The stainless steel barrel was a good deal more hygienic than the old wooden one. A hop in the glass said something about the way beer was produced in hole-in-the-corner, old-fashioned breweries that would no longer pass inspection. Area managers tried to contradict the heresy that their beer was a chemical product boosted with carbon dioxide, but the sheer ob-stina-cy of the beer drinker, who always stud-ied his pint before he swallowed it, prevailed. Even the big brewers had to acknowledge that the customer wasn't always wrong.

HILE THE WORKING horse powered most agricultural implements and pulled the wagon and the brewer's dray, blacksmiths were to be found in almost every rural parish. Not all of them worked in an idyllic world of ringing anvils and flying sparks. The romantic image of the blacksmith as a powerful, heavily muscled man was more fiction than fact. He was more likely to be a wiry individual with great stamina, who worked long hours and was always dehydrated by the heat of the forge. He was at the beck and call of

A Blacksmith

the farmers who waited impatiently for their teams to be shod or who had implements that needed continual re-fettling.

There were some smiths, a few who were not much more than show-smiths, farriers, others with intimate knowledge of the anatomy and the ailments of the heavy horse. Some of these 'horse doctors' knew as much as the vet and were consulted by the farming community to avoid the vet's fees. In general, smiths followed in the footsteps of their fathers and grandfathers from whom they inherited secrets of the trade, remedies for the sicknesses of horses and ponies, and ways of working, hardening and tempering metal.

Here and there the smith was more than a tradesman, and could fashion ornamental gates or make special ploughs for ploughing competitions. The really skilled smith could hand-weld and lay out a carpet of links to make chain harrows, forming the links one by one on the toe of the anvil.

When the working horse began to disappear some blacksmiths became mechanics and bought themselves welding outfits and compressors to provide an air blast when they used a forge, while others quickly advertised themselves as available for 'cold shoeing' and took their work out to pony stables.

O ONE CAN SAY FOR certain when and how the hybrid, common gamebird that is only here and there a truly wild bird, and generally a pampered creature looked after by keepers, came from the far east in the first place. The privilege of shooting it once depended on ownership of land, until a long succession of laws defining what game is, and what trespass in its pursuit amounts to finally brought a challenge allowing the ordinary man to shoot the pheasant if he had a licence and access to land on which the bird might be found. In the bad old days

Pheasant Shooting

even the great landowner was hard to put to it to fill his larder with pheasants. He lacked the kind of gun that would enable him to shoot more than one at a time. His weapon would be muzzle-loading, a flintlock perhaps, prone to the flash in the pan or letting the powder become damp. One at a time was 'good fishing', and this was all the sporting squire could hope for.

It wasn't until the nineteenth century that the battue was made possible by the invention of the breech-loading, double-barrelled shotgun. When it was further improved, the shooting gentleman began to stand at the side of the wood and have birds driven over him. This system was used everywhere to improve 'sport'. The pheasant was reared in ever-increasing numbers until bags of several hundreds were made by the great shots of the day using beautifully balanced ejectors that sometimes got almost too hot to handle. No one can say why such enormous bags of pheasants are killed. The bird costs a great deal more to rear and raise than the gamedealer or his customer could afford to pay for it.

THE WORLD OF JOHN Peel and the cry of his hounds in the morning was a much wilder one than that of Mr Jorrocks but a spectacle country folk have always enjoyed wherever there is a meet. Hunting is not really about killing foxes. It is a social occasion. The Master of the Hunt, with the advice of the huntsman and perhaps the keeper, as well as other estate servants, has already decided which cover will be drawn first. If no fox is found the pack will be rallied and bustle onto the next.

The Hunt

Cantering together, subscribers will exchange pleasantries and gossip, and perhaps arrive late to find the pack yelping and swarming over hillocks and through scrub because they have a faint, still lingering scent of Old Charlie. After a while a gate will be opened and the field will trot along the woodside, the heels of their mounts throwing up lumps of mud and small clods of grass while the wood echoes with the voices of hunt servants, 'Did you see him?' someone may ask; 'He gave us the slip! I saw him go over the hill just as we were closing the gate!' But imagination plays tricks. The huntsman blows his horn and the field is suddenly roused and moves from a jog to a positive canter and finally to a gallop. The old fox in the bracken slips off while the field pursues another that threads his way across country, his scent exciting hounds, but drifting, far off track.

This is what everyone came for, the fences, the ditches, the hard ride. A hunted fox doesn't turn back and takes another line if needs be. Fox-hunting is certainly not an efficient way of killing a fox. More foxes die of old age.

THE WILD GOOSE IN flight over the winter fields is a sight that stirs most people, for most of the wintering geese have come down from arctic regions to enjoy a milder climate than they would in the tundra.

They are a romantic sight to most people, welcome enough on the stubbles, but unwanted on the pasture. Ten geese may eat as much as a single sheep, depriving the sheep of nourishment, and driving the shepherd to despair. But the farmer has little time to stalk them when they settle. He knows how wary

Wild Geese

they are. The flock has a roster of sentinel geese that keep their heads high and warn the rest when danger is imminent. A man stalking the flock knows that if he doesn't keep down the geese will be in the air, sailing away, yelping their complaint, conversing with one another while a new field is looked for.

The omnivorous character of most of the goose family makes them as much at home on grass as on the tundra. They dibble and dabble to unearth the frosted carrot on the deserted vegetable field, and, when they have had their fill, rise in a trailing mass to find a roosting place far enough out on the open water or the exposed sands to keep them safe from harm until the following day.

They move as though they had a built-in, synchronised clock at the same time every morning and the same hour in the afternoon. They arrive in their wintering area on almost the same day each autumn, and depart in the same month each spring. If man wanted reassurance on the continuity of life and things unchanged, it is in the habit of geese that come and go, year after year, as they have done since the ice age.

HERE WAS A TIME WHEN the great landowners, more concerned with rearing pheasants and partridges than the welfare of their tenant farmers, forbade the harvesting of corn on their estates except with a sickle. A delayed harvest allowed ground birds to enjoy the grain and survive in fields of wheat or oats until the shooting season was properly under way. Things had to change of course, for Britain depended upon agriculture for its survival and its stability.

Soon the sickle and the scythe were put aside to make room for a corn reaper, a

The Corn Harvest

horse-drawn implement that left the wheat or oats in swaths to be lifted and tied by harvesters following behind. This gave place to the cornbinder, with a built-in conveyor belt which meant that the workers who followed no longer needed to lift and tie sheaves. Harvest was suddenly speeded up. The backache had been taken out of it all, even if more horses were needed to pull the cornbinder. The cornbinder had so many working parts and received such a hammering in the process of cutting corn that everyone knew it would one day have to be consigned to the scrap heap. Its days were numbered when the horses were put to grass and the old machine was hitched behind the tractor.

It might not have occurred to the farm labourer that when the horse went he would be the next to be made redundant but the harvest field was transformed overnight when the combine harvester trundled in to cut the wheat. The rickyard was never needed again. Straw was set alight on the stubbles. The grain went into a drying plant and then into a silo, while the man in the cab—most always a contractor's man—visored and masked, pursued his solitary way, alone and remote from the very corn he was cutting.

THE RED-LETTER day on the country calendar was always the local cattle show. Even when the motor-car came on the scene and the farmer could visit the agricultural show in the next county, and perhaps enter his prize milking cow to compete there in the dairy cattle class, he took less satisfaction in triumphing over someone he didn't know if he had won a smaller prize at the local show.

This competitiveness applies in every branch of husbandry. The man with a good flock or a fine herd needs

Cattle Shows

to know that it is as good as any he sees on his way to market. He takes a pride in his stock, his young gelding, his brood mare, his saddlebacks or his South Downs. When the local show is on he and his family, as well as his men, take a day off, dress themselves up and enjoy the occasion.

The term cattle show, which covered it all half a century ago, became inadequate when mechanisation came along, for now the makers of implements insisted on having their corner and displaying their wares. Everything the forward-looking farmer might need, and a lot of things he had little use for, was suddenly there on the five or six acres of the show field along with the free lunch and the beer tent.

No farmer ever likes to think he has the reputation of being behind the times. The show is where he discovers tomorrow's world, listens to his friends, falls for the spiel of the salesman, and buys the new machine. How much more enlightened he is than his poor old grandfather who wouldn't have bought that crawling juggernaut because he knew there was no future in such machines.

THE STAPLE DIET OF the majority of people today may be a fast food of some kind: frozen beefburgers, fish-fingers, and chips. Without doubt the potato figures prominently in the diet of not just the Irish, but the people of the British Isles as a whole.

It is a crop that can be grown in almost any kind of ground and there are literally thousands of tonnes of potatoes grown on small fields and parts of fields. The potato-grower of the fens has machinery for spinning the potato out of the furrow and grading it

The Potato Field

by size before it is mechanically bagged for the market. A man with only a few furrows digs his potatoes with the old-fashioned, broad-tined potato fork. The small farmer may have a potato-digger that will spin out the crop leaving the tubers on the surface to be gathered by potato-pickers engaged by the day. This, in fact, was the way even quite large potato fields were harvested at the beginning of the present century.

In autumn the potato haulms are wilted and brown. The purple-mauve blossom is long forgotten. Partridges dustbath along the furrows. Crows hang about to peck the exposed green tuber. The sun is warm, the scene a mellow one, and the furrows easily broken by the digger, drawn once upon a time by a single horse but now hauled by the tractor. There is nothing quite so satisfying as to unearth a potato from the furrow, put it in a bucket and carry the gathering to the sack at the end of the row. A kind of timelessness prevails. It seems that this was the way of things centuries ago. The potato-picker is in tune with all his peasant ancestors.

URDLE-MAKING as a country craft must go back to a distant past when the shepherd ceased to be an itinerant flockmaster, walking on and on with his sheep following him. In northern parts of Britain the shepherd in the hills constructed solid and permanent folds for his flock from the stone that lay all around him. In the rolling Downland as there is no stone to be quarried and carted and, since hazel grew in abundance in woodland areas, the trade of the hurdle-maker flourished.

The movable pen allowed a flock to

Hurdles for the Shepherd

be divided, manipulated, and fed on fresh ground when a particular area had become too trodden or over-manured. The hurdle-maker, well-acquainted with the shepherd's needs made his hurdle light, roughly three feet in height and six feet long. In order to keep them upright the framework incorporated holes into which pointed poles were inserted and driven into the ground. The hurdles were made where the coppice wood grew and, since only comparatively mature hazel would serve his purpose, the hurdle-maker had to have a considerable area of coppice available to him to keep him supplied with raw material. His hands and wrists needed to be very strong to enable him to turn and interweave the split rod through his framework of uprights standing on a basic spar or jig.

In addition to his work for shepherds the hurdle-maker still at the trade today occasionally finds a market for his wares when someone needs a stop-gap in a fence or gateway. Elsewhere the electric fence and the metal pen that can be transported in a truck may spell the end for one of our ancient country crafts.

ORRIS DANCING, AND the folklore attached to many rituals seen in different parts of the country, where groups of men in outlandish garb solemnly dance their dances and recite their ancient rhymes, are part of the traditional entertainment enjoyed in villages. Gartered and gaitered, these well-disguised country lads trip to and fro to the music of a mandolin or hurdy-gurdy while the rest of the village stares in wonder, laughs outright and applauds the more outrageous behaviour of individual members of the group.

Experts on the folklore and the cus-

Dancing on the Green

toms observed in different parishes are often able to give plausible explanations of the ritual, and the blacking of faces, the pattern of the dance, the superstitions involved, and the money demanded by the leader of the party of those appointed to collect dues from onlookers. The public loves to laugh and dance, just as the children of the village love the maypole, and the vicar must turn his blind eye on what is blatantly pagan, for doesn't he have the church decorated with the evergreen, holly and mistletoe at Christmas? Puritans finally put their foot down on morris men and their dancing, but in Henry VIII's reign it was part of the May festival in every rural parish.

The banning of the dance interrupted a pageant that had been introduced to Britain, it is said, by Edward I's queen. Thereafter it languished in obscurity until in our century there has been a great revival, with Morris dancing teams, schooled by enthusiastic members of the English Folk Dance Society, touring not only villages, but towns, to interest the general public in something that is part of our heritage. One result has been the formation of clubs and societies that compete with one another every year. Traditional things die hard, it is said, and dancing on the green dies hardest of all.

TIME WAS WHEN ROOK-eries were found in closer proximity to human habitation than they are now. Rooks seemed to like living close to man. They built in elm trees more than in any other sort of tree and, being gregarious by nature, they built close to one another, renovating the old nests in early spring and quarreling over sticks as well as the nest themselves.

Dutch elm disease came along and the old elms died. Very often the rooks detected the disease early on and moved to another clump of trees, perhaps a mile away, and with only a solitary cottage or

Rooks and Rookeries

farmstead for company. Or, where elms were lacking and the disease had deprived the birds of their favourite tree, hedgerow rookeries, with nests much nearer the ground than hitherto were to be found, were established. The habits of the rehabilitated rooks didn't change. They had their battles and squabbles. They fought, tumbled earthwards, and flew back to perch in high branches and complain, and every morning in the spring they departed in a happy throng, a cheerfully cawing tribe of rooks in search of a rootfield or cornfield. The rook is the most engaging member of the crow family because of this gregariousness. He can also be one of the greatest pests to a farmer with newly sown wheat or rows of young turnips. The rook pulls plants, one after another, but to no avail. The rook exacts a toll a farmer simply isn't prepared to pay. The farmer puts down his minute gun to frighten away foraging rooks. Then comes the rook shoot, a relentless slaughter of the half-fledged rooks perched round the nests in surviving rookeries. Hundreds of rooks are killed all over the country, the meat of their breasts made into rook pie.

SKATING, IT IS SAID, had its origin with Norsemen who fashioned bone skates which they lashed to their feet in order to travel comfortably on frozen lakes and rivers. Whether or not these primitive skates were the real prototype of the wood and metal skates imported from the low countries centuries later, skating was fashionable when lakes and fens were frozen. The river Thames didn't freeze over often enough, but the lake in St James's Park was known to do so on occasion and fashionable people liked to be seen on the ice. The fens of

Fen Skaters

East Anglia freeze more often, but nevertheless outdoor skating events have always been characterised by a certain spontaneity. For all of two hundred years the freeze has brought the people of Norfolk and Lincolnshire out to enjoy the spectacle, whether they are proficient skaters or possess no skates at all.

On these occasions the spectators stand and stare or slip and slide, breath steaming, their hands warmed by slapping their ribs. The experienced skaters glide here and there, swinging their arms professionally as they make tentative starts and short dashes along a wilderness of frost-petrified reeds. The novice wobbles out, falls and gets to his feet again to dust the frost from his clothes and reminds himself that he must keep out of the way of those conceited, completely coordinated people from the indoor rinks.

The enchantment lies in the fact that this is a natural, outdoor experience. It has the nostalgic magic of a Dickensian Christmas card: Elderly men stamp their feet and warm themselves with a nip from a flask. Mothers stand patiently waiting for their red-faced children to have had enough. This is a winter to be remembered, a kind of Lowry picture, carried in the mind, long after the last of the skaters has come off the ice with frost in crystals on his woolly hat and his cheeks and nose quite blue.

I N COUNTLESS VILLAGES dotted about rural England, often on a Sunday, and less frequently on Saturday, during summer, the sound of a bat hitting a cricket ball indicates that the English game is in progress. Village cricket is a very parochial and partisan affair, and something quite different from the kind of entertainment at Lords or on the sun-scorched pitches of Australia, India or Jamaica. Little has changed in a century so far as the village game is concerned. The spectators may be counted in tens on special occasions, never in hundreds. The

The Village Green and Cricket

atmosphere is friendly. Almost always the competing sides know one another by their first names. The club secretary and his wife concern themselves with refreshment and perhaps the scoreboard. Appeals against the light are infrequent. Umpires may have to take a little more criticism than those on the county ground, but they are used to it. They are somehow expected to be biased and partisan.

Village cricket has thriven wherever a side can be mustered. It is as much a feature of village life as the parochial church council, the parish council or the Women's Institute. It depends on the butcher, the baker, the candlestick-maker, the vicar and the postman who play year after year, enjoying not just the rivalry that exists between their own and the neighbouring village, but the whole social occasion, the bonhomie, the arguments in the bar after the match—something that is in the tradition of village life.

The village green, the church and the pub wouldn't be the same if the village couldn't field a side and keep up the tradition. Is it cricket, people ask, when the pitch is laid out on the very place where the bonfire was built, when boundaries are doubtful and lounging spectators get in the way? Would it be quite the same with everyone in whites and a computer scoreboard to keep tally?

HERE IS, THE BIBLE tells us, a time to reap and a time to sow, and in spring when most things are sown and planted the birds invariably take their toll. Rooks, crows, pigeons and even gamebirds follow the sower and the seed drill, picking grain that hasn't been covered by harrowing and rolling, or scratching to unearth the seed lovingly covered by the drill. In times long gone the sower strode the ploughed land as the great masters portrayed him, broadcasting corn with a deft movement of one hand after another. The sower's stride was even,

The Sowers Field

his rhythm perfect, or the corn would come up in bunches and there would be bare patches on the cultivated field. As surely as the sower sowed, the crows came sweeping in to feast on the grain, and small boys were employed as scarecrows, banging tins and rushing about to drive the birds away.

The sower was a rare individual in the rural community. Few men had the pace, the stature, the rhythm that was required, and to overcome this some rustic genius invented a little machine that came to be known as a fiddle. It was operated by a bow attached to a string that turned a wheel designed to scatter corn. 'Fiddling' his way over the ploughed field, the farmer could sow his own corn and not have to wait in line for the sower. On the cornfield he put up a scarecrow of straw and wood dressed in some of his own old clothes. Then the seed drill made the fiddle obsolete. The old straw and wood scarecrow was replaced by a mechanical one with a time fuse that allowed an explosion to take place at regular intervals during the day. The birds eventually became used to this machine, and the last resort would seem to be an 'inflatable man' who rears up from the field. This, one might think, could be the ultimate deterrent, but who can say?

ARES, UNLIKE RABBITS, come under the game laws. They are traditional animals of the chase, only to be hunted by the owner of the land and those to whom he may assign his right. In some parts of the country they have always been numerous and regarded as pests by farmers with little interest in the cultivation of game and shooting rights. Hare shoots are the order of the day in places overrun with hares, but the sporting gent has a strong aversion to wanton slaughter of hares and would have them hunted by hounds, coursed, or pursued by a pack of deep-

Hare Hunting

chested, short-legged, bustling beagles.

Coursing with greyhounds is not the most efficient way of catching a hare. The greyhound, fast as any other hunting hound, overruns its quarry, and the hare, wise in the art of survival, turns abruptly while the wretched greyhound, bewildered, looks about to discover where the hare has gone. The coursers have to cooperate with their charges to make sure that the hares are funnelled into a narrow avenue down which the hound can give chase. Beagles hunt like foxhounds, but, with shorter legs, bustle and fuss more, and mill round hillocks of gorse and bracken, taking the scent, bundling on and sometimes streaming off after a hare long gone through the next hedge and over the hill. Hares belong in their own small parish. Like the fox, they know the ground. When they are driven out of familiar places they don't know the escape routes. The master of the beagle pack knows the hill or the hollow where he has put up a hare for years and he knows, of course, that the startled hare will run in a circle and come back to the place on which he was born. Their dawdling in the bushes brought to an end by the huntsman and his assistants, the beagle pack trundles on to follow the hare round and round the fields.

Christopher Wormell is one of Britain's finest wood engravers. He has illustrated many books for adults and children, including *An Alphabet of Animals*, which won the Graphics Prize at the 1990 Bologna Book Fair.

Entirely self-taught, Wormell began engraving in 1982 and has won worldwide recognition as an illustrator. His works have been exhibited in the Victoria and Albert Museum. His other books include *Mowgli's Brothers*, the first story of Rudyard Kipling's *The Jungle Book*; *A Number of Animals*, which was featured on the 1993 New York Times list of books of the year;

and *Kitchen Wisdom* and *The Cook's Journal*, both from Running Press.

Wormell has a son and a daughter and lives in London.

ABOUT THE AUTHOR

Ian Niall writes on rural Britain for *Country Life* magazine. His other books include *The Poacher's Handbook*, *A Galloway Childhood*, and *Portrait of a Country Artist*.

He lives in Buckinghamshire.

This book has been bound using handcraft methods, and Smyth-sewn to ensure durability.

The dust jacket and interior were designed by Frances J. Soo Ping Chow.

The text was edited by Brian Perrin.

The text was set in Monotype Van Dijck.

The engravings by Christopher Wormell were cut in the end grain of boxwood with a burin, following the technique perfected by Thomas Bewick in the late eighteenth century.